Financially Fabulous Divas

(A First Time Car Buyer's Guide)

In the Driver's Seat

DEDICATION

This book is dedicated
to the many

Fabulous Women

who have touched my life in a positive way; women who helped mold me into the woman that I am today. They are the women with whom I share a bloodline. They are the women my mother calls friends; who have become my extended family.

They are my coworkers past and present. They are the nameless women who cross my path daily; women who make me smile and inspire me to do better. They are the special friends from my childhood: Connie, Lynn, and Marilyn; women with whom I share fond memories and lessons learned. They are the caring teachers from Grant School who saw the best in me.

They are the loving adults from my Miller Homes Community, "my village," that cared enough to chastise and nurture a young me. I will always hold a special place in my heart for Mrs. Margaret Mingo; one of the leaders of our neighborhood drill teams. Last, but not least, they are the women of Friendship Baptist Church who sprinkled me with love. In honor of my fabulous mother, Pauline Tyler, I raise my glass to toast the special divas that make me appreciate the solidarity among women. Salud.

TABLE OF CONTENTS

INTRODUCTION

The Allure: $99 Down $99 a Month Drive Away Today in Your Dream Car

They Call Me MR. GIMMICK!

I look good. I sound good, and I ooze sex appeal.

I have been told that I can be quite the charmer.

What can I say? *I am great at what I do.*

I roam freely through the advertisements and

often allude to things that are too good to be true.

I must admit that at times I can be shameless:

I will become whatever, or whoever, gets the job done.

Many beautiful damsels have succumbed to the tricks and

devices that I use to attract their attention.

Oh well, *it is not my fault if some take me at my word.*

It was their responsibility to decipher if what I ***implied*** *was*

fact or fiction.

They should have done their due diligence.

They should have searched for me in the fine print

where I dwell.

The **Dealership**

The Dealership

Hmm. I am not as naïve as he thinks. I know that up to means that he can offer me as little as $1.00 or "up to" as much as $5,000. I have done my research. I have learned to see through his gimmicks.

The Dealership

Looking Beyond the Gimmicks

When it comes to car buying, a diva is ready, willing, and determined to handle her business. She refuses to become the prey of a sly fox. Instead she travels through life with an open mind and is always eager to learn. She knows that a little information and effort can take the fear out of the car buying process.

The number one reason that women are taken advantage of is that they fail to do their homework. They expect the salesperson or the owner to give them a fair deal.

A diva, on the other hand, does not depend on the integrity of a *stranger*/salesperson. She does her research. She understands that the salesperson is there to handle business for him/herself and for the dealership.

The salespeople, managers, and even owners have their own living expenses. They may have rent or mortgages to pay. They may have their own car payments and families to feed. Selling cars or owning a dealership just happens to be the way they put food on the table.

Always remember that it is a business! Dealerships operate for the sole purpose of making money. It is *not* a social club and you are *not* there to make friends. You are there to handle business. No matter how nice the sales team is they have goals and quotas to meet. It is part of their job to be nice to you! They have a lot of cars to sell and selling *you* a vehicle gets them one sale closer to *their* goal. It gets them one sale closer to a better paycheck and/or a nice bonus.

The best customer for a car salesperson is the customer that lacks information and confidence in the car buying process. A customer that lacks confidence and especially information must trust and depend on the honesty of the salesperson and the dealership's management team.

The stakes are too high to walk into a dealership clueless and depend on someone else for a fair deal. The person that handles their business the best will walk away or drive away with the best deal: let that person be you.

A smart diva will not spend the entire day at a dealership. She will do most of the work long before she ever steps foot onto the lot, from checking the dealer's inventory, getting a copy of her credit report and knowing her credit score.

She knows how she is going to pay for the car. She knows how much she can afford to pay and how much the insurance is going to cost. A diva in the driver's seat understands there is more to the process than picking out a cute vehicle, buying new mats, and/or hanging up a car freshener.

Chapter 1

Silly Boys, Car Buying Is for Girls!

The Allure

EXTRA, EXTRA, READ ALL ABOUT IT!

Good Credit! Bad Credit! No Credit!

NO PROBLEM!

$99 Down* Payments as low as $99 a Month*

$5,000 Minimum for Your Trade *

Push it - Pull it - Drag it - Tow it

Just Get It Here!

ENTER TO WIN!

Bring in Your Winning Key!

If your key starts the engine you will Drive Away Today in your Dream Car*

Don't Believe the Hype!

Ladies, be leery of brightly colored advertisements (Ads) offering deals that seem too good to be true. Consider this and be honest. How can it be possible for a person to have bad/limited credit, no money for a down payment and *still* qualify for an expensive vehicle with low monthly payments? The odds are that it is not possible.

If you have a low credit score, or no credit history you should be prepared to bring more money to the table. When shopping for a vehicle you should avoid tent sales, inventory reduction sales, bank sales, finance parties, and of course the popular *tax return specials*.

The circus like atmosphere, the balloons, the popcorn machines and free soft drinks are just distractions used to deter you from thinking clearly. This could easily lead to purchasing a car on a whim without careful consideration and research. People often go to these "*Special Sales*" anticipating a great deal, only to find themselves talked into purchasing a vehicle with hidden fees, high interest rates and years of payments.

The main purpose of auto ads offering unrealistic deals is to attract as many potential buyers into the dealership as possible. The first lesson in the car business is that selling cars is a numbers game. If they can increase the number of people that flock into the dealership, they increase their odds of selling us a vehicle.

It is like a man with a bad pickup line. If he uses the same bad line on enough women, he increases his odds of one of us falling for it. When it comes to the car buying process most of us will overlook the asterisk or other pointer symbols directing us to the fine print, and the *truth* within the ad/ gimmick.

The problem starts when we get to the dealership with our bad credit and empty wallets. That is when the salesperson points to the bottom of the ad and asks you if you read the *fine print.* He/she tells you that those offers only apply to people **With Approved Credit**, which is the meaning of the **W.A.C.*** in the ad that you overlooked. The salesperson wants to know if you have excellent credit. He/she informs you that although your credit is not so great, with $2,000 or $3,000 down, he can still get you into a nice vehicle.

You tell him that you are unable to come up with the $2,000 or $3,000 needed to buy a vehicle. He pretends to think for a moment then he says: "Let me ask you a question: is there anyone in your family who loves you and cares enough about you to cosign a loan for you?" "Maybe my grandmother," you tell him. He points to a chair in his office and tells you to sit down and he will give your grandmother a call.

The Dealership

Purchasing a vehicle is the largest purchase for most people *second only* to purchasing **a home**: take your time and learn as much as possible about the car buying process. If you have bad credit and can wait until you increase your score you can save yourself hundreds or even thousands of dollars in interest. Of course, another option is to always save your money, shop for a less expensive vehicle, and purchase it with cash.

The Dealership

The Dealership

Chapter 2

Forget What a Man Wants! What Does a Lender Want?

Forget What a Man Wants! What Does a Lender Want?

What do lenders want? Short, sweet and to the point: lenders want their money back *and* to earn a profit for lending you money. Lenders do not know most of the people that come to them needing or wanting to borrow money. The only information they have about us is what they see before them in black and white. They must determine from our credit report, our financial paper trail, and work history how likely we are to repay the loan.

If you go to a bank or credit union to borrow money, they want to see in black and white what makes you worthy of a line of credit or a loan. They do not care how well dressed you are, how nice a person you are, or how great a mother you may be. They do not care if you have children depending on you. They want you to prove – *again in black and white* – just how likely you are to repay the loan. They want to know what you are bringing to the table other than good looks, charm, or a sad story.

Lenders want to know if you have bankruptcies, liens or judgments against you. They want to know the length of your credit history and what types of credit you have such as: student loans, credit cards, home loans, etc. They are also interested in your **debt-to-**

income ratio (how much you *owe* compared to how much you *earn*).

Whether we like it or not, financial institutions tend to lend money to people who do not need their money. These are people who ***own*** items that are worth more than they are trying to borrow such as; real estate, jewelry, stocks, bonds, income property, etc.

The second group that lenders like to do business with is people who ***earn*** or receive enough money to repay the loan. This group also has a history of repaying their debt.

If a potential borrower does not own anything of financial value or earn enough money to repay the loan then a ***cosigner*** may be required to be responsible for the loan. This may also include people who lack experience with credit or the credit is in their spouse/partner's name.

To get started with the car loan process most lenders will require documents such as:

- **Proof of Income**
  Pay Stubs, Tax Returns, etc.

- **Proof of Residence**
  A Valid Driver's License, Mortgage Statement, Lease Agreement, Utility Bills, Bank

Statement, Social Security Card, Credit Card Statement, etc.

- **Vehicle Information**
  Year, Make, Model, Vehicle Identification Number (also known as a VIN number), Mileage, Purchase Price, etc.

- **Proof of Car Insurance**
  Full Coverage Insurance is required if the vehicle is being financed.

- **Credit Report**

Lenders will normally get started by checking your **credit score** and pulling your **credit report**.

What is a Credit Score?

A credit score, also known as a **FICO** (Fair Isaac Corporation) score, is a three-digit number that is calculated based on your credit/payment history. It ranges from **300 to 850.**

For example:

- 300-650 Poor
- 651-700 Fair
- 701-759 Good
- 760-850 Excellent

(Note: There is also another score called a Vantage Score. A Vantage Score can range from 501 to 990 but may not reflect your true score).

The purpose of your Credit Score is to help lenders determine if they should extend credit or lend money to you. Once again, the lender wants to have an idea of just how likely you are to repay their money. Your score will also determine how much you pay for a loan (interest rate). A low score may mean that you are too much of a risk, and your loan request could be denied.

Five factors determine your Credit Score; the two most important factors are your payment/credit history and how much you currently owe.

- **Thirty-five percent (35%)** of your credit score is based on your **payment history**. Your payment history shows a creditor if you have a habit of paying your bills late or on time. It tells a creditor if you have bills that you have **not** paid and been sent to collection agencies. It also shows creditors if you've had a car or other item repossessed because you failed to pay. A bankruptcy in your history will also hurt your score.

- **Thirty percent (30%)** of your credit score is based on your **outstanding debt**: Your outstanding debt is how much you owe on your credit cards, an auto loan, or your home loan/mortgage.

- **Fifteen percent (15%)** of your credit score is based on **how long you've had credit**. (How many years you've had your credit card – or how long you've been making payments on an auto loan).

- **Ten percent (10%)** of your credit score is based on the **number of inquiries**. Each time you fill out an application to borrow money (loan) or apply for a credit card *you* are giving a bank or financial institution permission to check your credit report. The credit bureaus keep a record of those inquiries.

- **Ten percent (10%)** of your credit score is based on the **types of credit** that you have such as; student loans, credit cards, auto or home loans/mortgage, etc.

What is a Credit Report?

A credit report is an intimate look at the way you handle your money. Think of it as a financial *report card* from the lenders that you borrowed money from, or lenders who have extended you credit. It includes your **past** and **current** credit activities. This report includes your account balances and shows if you make payments on time.

Your credit report will also show if any action was taken against you for unpaid bills. It will show if you did not pay a debt and your account was sent to a collection agency, or if a creditor took back property (such as a car) for non-payment.

What is in Your Credit Report?

The format may be different, but credit reporting agencies supply the same categories of information:

Identifying Information

Your name and any aliases

Your current and previous addresses

Your social security number and date of birth

Your employment information

These items on your credit report are updated with information that you supply to lenders. This information does not affect your credit score.

<u>Trade Lines/Credit Accounts</u>

Each time you open and establish an account with a lender, the lending institution reports a number of things to credit reporting agencies:

The type of accounts you opened: i.e.; credit card, auto loan, student loan, mortgage, etc.

The date you opened or closed the account;

The amount of the loan (example: $15,000 car loan) or the amount of your credit limit;

The account balance and your payment history.

The report also includes a list of **late** payments that were 30, 60, 90 or 120 plus days late.

<u>Credit Inquiries</u>

Each time you apply for a loan or credit card, you authorize a lender to ask for a copy of your credit report. The inquiries section contains a list of those lenders. Giving a lender permission to view your credit report should only be done when you are ready and able to do business with that institution. Your credit report contains important and valuable information and should not be given out lightly.

Public Record Information

Public records are also shown in your credit report. State and county records, information on tax liens, bankruptcies, or monetary judgments are included.

FREE CREDIT REPORT

Once a year, by U.S. law, you are entitled to request a FREE copy of your credit report. Beware! Many companies charge a fee for this information when it is available to you for *FREE*.

There are three main credit reporting bureaus:

1. TransUnion
2. Experian
3. Equifax.

To receive your free copies, contact each of the three main credit bureaus by phone, mail, or go to the official website at **www.annualcreditreport.com.**

Be prepared; find out in advance what documents are required for the loan. Being proactive can save you time and multiple trips to the dealership or lender.

Chapter 3

Really! 7 Years to Pay for a Car!

The True Cost of S-t-r-e-t-c-h-i-n-g Out Your Payments

The Dealership

The Scent of a Car

We all love that new car smell. At least we love that artificial "*chemically-induced*" new car smell. We cannot trade 5, 6, or especially 7 years of hard work and monthly payments for the scent of a car. A car is not an investment and will continue to go down in value.

Keep in mind that the dealerships pay professionals to detail every inch of the vehicles on their lots. After all, a polished vehicle makes a much better impression than the dirty vehicles many buyers leave behind. Do not fall in love with a cleaned-up version of one of those discarded cars.

Chasing Low Payments

Before you visit the dealership do a little research. Information is power and can save you money. A few questions you should answer before heading to the dealership. How do you plan to pay for your car? Can you afford to pay cash? Do you have money for a down payment? Will you need to borrow money to purchase a vehicle?

How is your credit? Before you commit yourself and your future earnings (money that you have not earned yet) to 5, 6 or even 7 years of monthly payments, consider the reality of such an obligation. If you need **84 months** to pay for a car the reality is that you are buying a vehicle that is beyond your means.

Stretching your payments out for a longer period may seem like a good idea. You get your "*dream car*" with what feels like affordable payments. Life is good…until you want to trade in your car for a newer model or your family grows, and you *need* a larger vehicle.

By making small payments with little or no money down you increase your chances of becoming "upside down" on your loan, also known as negative equity. This means that you owe more money on the car than it is worth. For example, you owe $20,000 and your car is only worth $13,000. With negative equity in your vehicle, it will be more difficult and more expensive to qualify for a new loan.

No matter what advertisers or our neighbors tell us, we are not what we drive! Think long and hard before committing years and thousands of dollars to the purchase of a car. Vehicles depreciate by about 25% to 40% the moment you drive off the lot.

We would never consider walking past a trash can and tossing in money or our paycheck. Yet we think nothing of investing years of making payments to purchase a vehicle that will only decrease in value. If a loan is your only option, you should aim to own your car outright in 3 years or less.

A diva knows to keep a safe and reliable vehicle for as long as possible. She understands the financial freedom of not having a monthly car payment. The money she saves monthly can be used to attack other debt. It is also money that can be used to fund an emergency account or retirement account.

The Power of Knowledge

- We live in the age of information. Take advantage of all the information at your disposal. Take the time to research car-buying tips. You can be sure the salespeople and finance officers are taking classes on how to make the most money for themselves and the dealership.

- Shop around and compare models and prices. Do not allow your credit report to be pulled while you are just browsing. Each time your credit report is pulled your credit score is reduced.

- Know how much you can afford to spend for a vehicle. Salespeople are trained to distract you from the price of the car and get you to focus only on the payment. **Do not be a payment buyer.** A payment buyer knows very little about the car buying process and focuses only on the payment amount. You should know the price and more importantly the value of the car that you are considering.

- How much is the car that you are pondering worth? How much is your trade worth? Use the Kelley Blue Book or the N.A.D.A book which stands for the National Automobile Dealers Association to get an idea of the value of the car you are considering *before* you purchase or trade your vehicle.

- Remember you are responsible for the remaining balance on your trade. If you owe $8,000 on your trade and the dealer gives you $5,000, the remaining $3,000 will be rolled over or added to your new loan.

- Come to an agreement on a fair price for the car you want to purchase. Do not pay the sticker price. Let the salesperson know that you do not want to discuss payments until you agree on a purchase price.

- While working at a car dealership I met a couple who told the salesperson how much they wanted to pay monthly for a vehicle. Because the couple did not know the price of the car, or their credit score, the finance manager was able to increase the price of the car to match the payment they wanted.

- Be careful about signing a contract with low payments that include a "balloon payments". It may be possible to have low payments for years and a final balloon payment near the end of your contract. The problem is that the balloon payment can be so expensive that you may not be able to afford the payment and lose your vehicle.

For example:

With a **balloon payment** in your contract, you may have monthly payments as low as $250 a month with a final balloon payment due near the end of your contract for as much as $10,000.

- When buying a *used* car be sure to research the history of the vehicle. If you do not ask, the salesperson is not required to reveal the history of the car or if it has been in an accident.

- Request a **Carfax**. A Carfax history report checks for such things as:

    - Title problems
    - The number of owners
    - Severe accidents reported, flooding
    - Frame damage
    - If the car was reported as a total loss
    - If air bags were deployed
    - Service record
    - If it was a rental
    - If it was purchased at an auction
    - If it was a fleet car

(A fleet car is an inexpensive vehicle purchased by a company or organization for their employees to use, normally salespeople).

While it is a good idea to request a Carfax report, do not allow it to give you a false sense of security.

A Carfax report will not give you information about the condition of the car.

- **Hire a mechanic** that you trust to inspect the vehicle that you are considering **before** you buy the vehicle! Also, talk with the mechanic about parts and labor. There can be a huge difference in repair cost depending on the make and model of the vehicle you choose.

  My youngest daughter paid a mechanic a reasonable fee to inspect a used vehicle **before** she made her final decision. As a result, the car she was considering had a serious oil leak and needed about $3,000 worth of repairs. Needless to say, she did not buy that car. The dealership knew about the oil leak, but chose not to disclose any problem.

- It is important to **have a mechanic inspect the vehicle** before you sign the **"AS IS CONTRACT".** It is worth the price to find out ahead of time if the car you are considering needs major work. Do not fall in love with a car and become blind to the mechanics it.

Once you sign the "**as is**" contract, it is binding even if there are unknown problems. In most states there is no lemon law, no 3-day right to cancel or buyer's remorse clause on used cars.

If possible, **secure financing** ahead of time. Once you find the car that you want to purchase, check with your financial institution about financing.

- Research **auto insurance** rates **before** making your final decision. You should get at least three different price quotes before choosing an insurance company.

  I once sold a car to a young man, whose car note was $275, and his insurance payments were $520 a month. He was only 22 and the two-door car he purchased was considered a sports car. *His monthly insurance payment did not include Gap insurance.*

- **What is Gap insurance?** The proper term for Gap insurance is Gap Coverage, it is also known as Guaranteed Auto Protection. In the event of a total loss, Gap insurance will cover the difference between the *current book value* of a vehicle and the loan *amount owed* on the vehicle.

For example:

If you owe the lender $20,000 for your vehicle but the current book value of the vehicle is only $13,000, Gap insurance would cover the difference or the **Gap** between the two amounts (in this case it would be $7,000).

Anyone owing more money on his or her car loan than the car is worth should consider investing in Gap insurance.

- Another possible cost when you purchase a vehicle is **property tax**. Some states charge property tax when you purchase a new or pre-owned vehicle. Remember to check on property tax for your state (not the same as sales tax). Do not be surprised by an unexpected bill a few months after you purchase your vehicle.

- Eventually all vehicles will need some type of repair work, or just basic maintenance, to keep them running smoothly. Those **repairs** can easily cost hundreds of dollars. It is a good idea to prepare for those repairs ahead of time by saving a little money in an emergency fund.

- Do not sign a **bill of sale** with blanks or contracts that read "subject to bank approval." Dealers will sometimes allow you to take the vehicle home before the bank approves the loan allowing you to believe that the deal is complete.

- If you receive a call from your salesperson to return to the dealership to "re-sign" your paperwork because the original loan request was not approved or fell through be sure to compare the **contracts**. You have the right to have your trade returned and start from the beginning with a new contract.

- Get all verbal promises in writing and signed by an *authorized* manager.

- Retrieve your keys after they complete the test drive and assessment on your trade. Some salespeople will pretend to "misplace" your keys to prevent you from leaving, trying to give themselves a little more time to convince you to buy a car.

- If you trade in a car that has a balance, make sure the dealer puts in writing that they will pay off your trade within 10 days. I sold a car to a couple who traded in their car and the dealership took three months to pay off the balance. Because the car was still in the couple's names, they continued receiving delinquent payment calls and letters from the loan company.

- Remember: know what your trade is worth ahead of time.

If you are just looking, do not give your telephone number to the salesperson unless you want to receive calls for the next year. When they have a slow period, they will look through their old numbers and make **cold calls** (randomly calling old contacts about the possibility of buying a car).

- Important note: Never sign anything without first reading, understanding and accepting the terms of the contract.

What you should know before signing the contract:

The number of months/years you will make payments, the annual percentage rate (APR), and the name of the primary borrower if it is a joint loan, the final cost of the loan including, interest, tax, warranty, fees, and any add-ons. Also, check to be sure there is not a balloon payment in the contract.

- Take your time, read the contract and sleep on the decision. Do not be pressured into purchasing a vehicle on the spot. You have the right to take your time and even walk away from a deal.

- The final cost of the vehicle is the **term:** number of months the car is financed multiplied by the monthly payment.

For example:

Monthly payment $300
Term/number of months you will make payments 60
$300 (monthly payment) x 60 (number of payments) = $18,000

- If you stop making payments as agreed, you are in default and the lender has the right to **repossess**/take back the vehicle. Remember the vehicle does not legally belong to you until you make the final payment. Know how much you can afford and stick to your budget.

- Even if you voluntarily return a vehicle, it is *still* considered repossession and it will lower your credit score.

Note:

Keep in mind that your car payments will come out of your **disposable income** and *not* your **gross income**. Some lenders will give you a false sense of buying power by focusing on your gross income.

What is Gross Income?

Your gross income is your total earnings **before** taxes, retirement plans/401k, and other similar deductions. Your **net income** is your take-home pay followed by **disposable income**.

What is Disposable Income?

Disposable income is money used for your necessary living expenses such as rent/mortgage, food, utilities, **car note**, *plus* debt that you are legally responsible for repaying, also known as bills.

DO NOT FALL for LINES Such As:

- "I am trying to help you rebuild your credit. The only way to rebuild your bad credit is to purchase a car and have it financed." This statement is not true; you do not need to purchase a car to rebuild your credit.

- "They just sold the car in the advertisement, but we have another great car that is just a little more expensive." This is known as the "Bait and Switch" move. A gimmick to get you to come into the dealership.

- "The payments are high, but if you pay on time for six months you can refinance your car with us and get lower payments." Do not believe it unless they are willing to put it in writing, which they are not. Do not pay more than you can comfortably afford.

- "Today is the last day to take advantage of that price."

- "We have another buyer interested in purchasing this car." If they do have another buyer, there will always be other cars.

- "We need to keep your trade overnight to assess the value." These are just tactics to put you in their vehicle overnight hoping that you fall in love with the car, increasing the chances that you will purchase it. Salespeople are often encouraged to get the customer to "*fall in love*" with the vehicle.

- "It is less expensive to purchase a warranty from the dealership." In reality, the markups on warranties are almost double at some dealerships. I no longer purchase the warranties because they never covered my repairs. Instead, I put money into an emergency fund for when I need car repair. You should do your own research and do what is best for you.

  "Everything, and I do mean everything, is covered under this warranty; from bumper to bumper!" Only believe what is in writing.

- "You are required to purchase life insurance from the dealership or a warranty to get the loan." Not true. You have the right to purchase life insurance and/or a warranty from an outside company.

.

The Dealership

The man, the myth, the mechanic

"Having your oil changed on a regular basis is one of the most important things you can do to keep your car in proper running order."

-Charles Hopkins

Chapter 4

The Finance Office: Revealing the Secret Back-End Sales that go on Behind Closed Doors

The Finance Office

"If you think nobody cares if you're alive, try missing a couple of car payments."

-Earl Wilson

The Last Stop
The Finance Office

The last step in the car buying process is the finance office. This is where you will need to pull out your reading glasses and your calculator. Before you enter the finance office, you should have a good idea of the total cost of your vehicle. The total should include the price of your vehicle, state tax, tags, fees, add-ons, and the cost for financing (fees vary by state). Your salesperson can give you the basic numbers. Find out the interest rate before entering the finance office.

****

The two ways dealerships make profits are:

1. ***Front-End Sales***
2. ***Back-End Sales.***

The Finance Office *is where the secret* ***back-end*** *sales take place.*

Front-end profits are the gains made from the actual sale of the vehicle. The **front-end** profits occur before you enter the finance office.

<u>For example</u>:

If you pay $20,000 for a vehicle and the vehicle cost the dealership $18,000, the profit for the dealership is $2,000.

$20,000 - $18,000 = $2,000 profit

What Are Back-End Sales?

Back-End Sales are the items the finance manager will try to sell you such as:

- Warranties
- Maintenance contract
- Paint and fabric protection
- Window etching
- Gap Insurance, etc.

Do not be intimidated by the finance and insurance manager. He or she will not be making your payments for you. Sometimes it is comforting to have a good friend or family member with you for support. Under no circumstance do you sign the contract without reading it from top to bottom. Flip it over to make sure there is nothing on the back of the contract. Search the contract for "add-ons."

I went with my daughter to the dealership when she purchased her SUV. Satisfied with the vehicle, the price, the interest rate and the monthly payment we went on to the finance office. She informed the salesperson that she did not want her payments to exceed $300 (never do what she did). Once inside the finance office I noticed that the final total on the contract was more than $4,000 higher than the total that I figured. It turned out that the finance manager "added on" an oil change package, insurance and a warranty to the contract without my daughter's consent for an additional $4,200.

The finance manager kept the amount slightly above my daughter's target payment of $300. When it comes time to sign your contract, look beyond the payment. The finance manager said to me "most people just sign the contract without reading it." He apologized for the "misunderstanding" and removed the insurance and warranty from the contract (she decided to keep the gap insurance). Reading the contract reduced her monthly payments by $50 and saved her $3,500.

Remember, have a copy of your credit history and know your credit score. Knowing your credit score will help you find the credit tier that you should fall under and give you an idea of the interest rate you should qualify for ahead of time. Make sure your credit report is accurate before doing business.

The better your credit and the closer the car is to the invoice for a new car or book value on a used car the lower your financing rate.

If you are interested in buying a warranty, know what it covers and what it *does not* cover, *before* you make the purchase.

Beware of *"menu" add-ons*. This happens when the finance manager groups add-ons into packages and gives them fancy names such as, *the supreme package* or *the golden tier*. These menu add-on packages can increase your monthly payment by $30, $60, or $90. An additional $90 on a 60-month loan is more than $5,000. The finance manager is counting on you choosing one and not thinking about the cost. It is okay to say no!

Payment calculators are available online. Once you know your credit score and credit tier, a payment calculator can give you an idea of the monthly payment you can expect.

A New Vehicle: Trading Up
"Once upon a time…"

I wanted to buy a new car and trade in my old vehicle, but I was told that I owed too much money on my old vehicle. What does that mean? Being upside down on your auto loan means that you owe the lender more money than your vehicle is worth. I make my payments on time. How could this happen?

Let's go back to the beginning. The advertisement that caught your eye read, "At least $3,000 for your trade! Push it, pull it, or tow it." It was not necessary for you to push, pull, or even tow your car to the dealership, but it was starting to give you trouble. The $3,000 that they promised for your trade would make an attractive down payment toward a newer vehicle. The trouble starts because you still owe the bank $6,000 on your old vehicle. You found a car that you love with a sticker price of $20,000.

Sticker Price ....$20,000.

Balance on Trade ....6,000. (You are responsible for the remaining balance on trade.)

Dealer Fee ....500. (Dealerships may charge fees.)

Property Tax ....300. (The tax may be higher in other states.)

Auto Tags....................50. (Charges vary by state.)

Warranty ....4,500. (Different prices and warranty choices)

Gap Insurance ....+ 800.

Sub-Total....................$32,150.

Trade Allowance........$- 3,000.

Loan Amount ....$29,150.

This does not include interest!

We always hear how cars lose value as soon as you pull off the lot. So, if your $20,000 car loses 25% when you pull off the lot, it is now worth $15,000.

***You owe $29,150 plus interest on your new car.**

***Your new car is now worth $15,000**!

That is how we become upside down in our car loan.

Car Insurance

Car insurance is regulated at state level. All states have laws regarding the *minimum* car insurance coverage that you **must** have to legally drive your car.

What Is Liability Insurance?

Liability insurance covers damage that *you* cause to other people and their property with your car. Liability insurance **does not** cover damage to *your* vehicle.

<u>For example</u>:

If you back into someone's car and cause a thousand dollars' worth of damage your liability insurance will cover the repair work on the *other* person's vehicle. Your liability insurance will not cover any damage to *your* car.

As the **policyholder or insured** you will be responsible for paying the **deductible** before the insurance company will pay the claim. If your deductible is $500, the insurance company will pay the remaining $500, but only *after* you pay your portion.

An **insurance claim** is a formal request to an insurance company asking for a payment based on the term of the insurance policy.

Full Coverage Insurance

The term full coverage is a little misleading. There is *not* one policy that covers everything-instead there are combinations of different insurance policies.

Full Coverage Insurance is state *required* liability or no-fault insurance *plus* other insurance policies such as collision, comprehensive, uninsured, underinsured, gap insurance, etc.

- **Collision** covers your vehicle in the event of an accident (required if the vehicle is being financed).

- **Comprehensive** covers vandalism, theft, and other damages that are not the result of an accident (optional).

- **Uninsured** insurance will cover you and the people in your car if you are in an accident with someone who does not have liability insurance. This insurance covers medical bills but *does not* cover damage to your vehicle (optional).

- **Underinsured** insurance protects you against drivers that have low liability insurance limits. This insurance pays over the other driver's limit (optional).

Insurance Score

How much can I expect to pay for Car Insurance?

How much you pay for car insurance will depend in large part on your Insurance Score. Keep in mind when you hear the insurance quote that most companies only offer a six-month policy.

What is an Insurance Score?

An **Insurance Score** is a rating that is computed and used by insurers. Since insurance companies are in business to make money they want to reduce their chances of paying claims. Your score represents the likelihood of you filing an insurance claim.

How is my Score Determined?

Your insurance score is based on your overall credit rating and your history of insurance claims. It seems that people with higher credit scores tend to file fewer insurance claims.

Do you have a heavy foot and love to drive fast? If so, you may want to slow down if you value your money, *and your life*. The average cost of a speeding ticket is $150. Your driving record/history plays a major role in the amount you will pay for insurance (laws vary by state).

If you have a clean driving record with no accidents or moving violations you may qualify for a lower rate-many insurance companies offer a **safe driver discount**. Insurance company's offer different types of discounts so be sure to ask questions. Another factor in determining your insurance rate is your annual driving mileage. The average person drives about 15,000 miles a year. If you only drive around your town and fall under the average, you may qualify for a **low-mileage discount**.

Do you lack patience and only s-l-o-w down when approaching a stop sign? If so you may want to reconsider that bad habit. That move is referred to as a "*rolling stop*" and *is* a traffic violation in some states.

- The higher your insurance score the lower your premiums/payments (770 or higher is considered a good score).

- The lower your insurance score the higher your premiums (500 or lower is considered a poor score).

- The Insurance scores range is 200-997.

Do your research and respect the traffic laws. You do not want to pay traffic tickets and/or higher than necessary insurance rates. Enjoy the road and be safe.

notes

notes

notes

notes

notes

notes

Made in the USA
Monee, IL
13 September 2026

62981882R00046